ALL THINGS OCTOPUSES FOR KIDS

FILLED WITH PLENTY OF FACTS, PHOTOS, AND FUN TO LEARN ALL ABOUT OCTOPUSES

ANIMAL READS

THIS BOOK BELONGS TO...

_____

_____

WWW.ANIMALREADS.COM

CONTENTS

Welcome to the World of Octopuses!   1
What is an Octopus?   5
Different Octopus Species   11
History of the Octopus   29
Characteristics and Appearance   35
The Life Cycle of an Octopus   55
Befriend Octopuses!   63
Thank You!   67

WELCOME TO THE WORLD OF OCTOPUSES!
SMART AND SQUISHY COLOR-CHANGING CREATURES

Lurking in the darkest reaches of our planet's oceans lives an animal known as the master of disguise. This incredible, ninja-like creature can change color to camouflage with its surroundings. It can also change its body's shape to fit through the smallest nooks and crannies of seabed rocks and even change their texture. It can pounce upon unsuspecting prey in the blink of an eye...

What is this most fascinating and clever trickster?

The octopus, of course!

Octopuses are among the most entrancing and mysterious animals on our planet. Aside from their utterly bizarre bodies, they showcase incredible intelligence – they can solve complex problems and then remember the solutions.

Octopuses are also known to be one of the oldest living creatures on our planet. *How long, exactly?* Nobody knows with *100% certainty*. Octopuses are as mysterious as the oceans themselves.

Despite our immense technological and scientific advances, the octopus is still one tentacle-length ahead of us humans.

Intrigued to know more?

Glad you are!

Then join us as we dive into the world of mystical sea creatures and soak in all we can learn about the incredible octopuses.

WHAT IS AN OCTOPUS?

You might already know that the octopus is one of the weirdest-looking animals in the world, right? *Well, there's more where that came from!* Octopuses are part of the **Cephalopoda** (*pronounced sefalopoda*) animal family, a group of creatures whose head is directly connected to their limbs.

That's what Cephalopoda means in Greek: **literally 'head foot'!**

The cephalad family includes various kinds of octopus, squid, and cuttlefish. All share common traits, aside from the bizarre head-foot shape. They are all **bilaterally symmetrical** – which means the left half and right half are absolutely identical.

Bilaterally = *something that involves both sides*

Symmetrical = *exactly similar on two opposing sides*

The word octopus also derives from the Greek, from two separate words that mean '*eight feet.*'

As mentioned, octopuses are incredibly intelligent and resourceful, yet scientists don't yet know how they manage all their clever tricks. They are color-blind, for example, yet still manage to change their own color to blend in with their environment. Octopuses have also been observed taking things apart for the sheer curiosity and fun of it all.

So, what are some basic facts we know about octopuses?

Well, we know that they lay eggs – *tons of eggs at once* – and are equipped with an ink sac. The octopus squirts ink to distract and irritate predators, so it can make a quick getaway.

Most species of octopus live alone, and the males, unlike the females, have a pretty short life span. Octopuses are known for having blue blood, eight arms, no skeleton, three **(yes, three)** hearts, and nine brains.

Whaaaaat?

Just wait ... soon you'll know more!

There's a ton of stuff we know about octopuses and even more that we don't. This is what makes them one of the most fascinating animals to study!

WHAT LOOKS LIKE HALF AN OCTOPUS?

The other half!

DIFFERENT OCTOPUS SPECIES

OCTOPUSES COME IN ALL SHAPES AND SIZES...

There are over 300 different species of octopuses that we know about. *And guess what?* Scientists think there may be more that we have not discovered yet. That's because the octopus lives at considerable ocean depth – they mainly crawl along sea beds, so there are probably more deep-dwelling species that humans have yet to come across.

The most notable difference between all the species of octopuses is their size. In fact, it's hard to think of another animal group that has so much variety when it comes to size.

The most giant octopus ever recorded weighed 600 lbs. and had an arm span of 30 feet! The smallest known octopus species is only 1 inch long and weighs just one gram.

Now let's go ahead and meet eight of the coolest types of octopuses in the oceans today.

THE GIANT PACIFIC OCTOPUS

This octopus is the largest of all the species. *Remember that 600 lb. octopus earlier?* That huge fella was one of these guys. Giant Pacific Octopuses live deep in the ocean, around 400 feet below the surface. They mostly love to hang out along the coast of the western United States and Canada, as well as along the coasts of Russia, Japan, and Korea.

Like most other octopuses, the Giant Pacific lives a solitary life. Their favorite meals include squid, lobster, shrimp, fish, and even smaller octopuses. When it's time to reproduce, Giant Pacific Octopuses, like all others, lay eggs. But these octopuses put chickens to shame. **A female can lay 90,000 eggs at a time!**

Giant Pacific Octopuses live much longer in the wild than other species. However, this still isn't a very long time. The average life span for this species is 3-5 years.

THE BLUE-RINGED OCTOPUS

On the opposite end of the size chart is the Blue-ringed Octopus. Although tiny at just 8 inches in size, this species is one of the most poisonous types of octopus around and carries tetrodotoxin, the same kind of venom as poison dart frogs.

Found in small tide pools, shallow waters, and coral reefs from Japan to Australia, these small octopuses produce a deadly toxin when they bite that is strong enough to kill 26 adults!

Thankfully, these octopuses are chill and don't typically bite anyone except for their favorite food of crustaceans, like small shrimp and krill. But if you see a small yellow octopus with blue and black rings all over its body, steer clear!

You just might have found the deadly but adorably cute, Blue-ringed Octopus.

DUMBO OCTOPUS

If you've ever seen the Disney movie by the same name, you can probably already imagine what is special about the Dumbo Octopus. **That's right!** Members of this unusual-looking octopus family have two large floppy "*ears*" that stick out on their heads. These "ears" are actually fins that they use to swim, much like the Disney elephant used its ears to fly.

There are actually 15 different kinds of Dumbo Octopuses that we know about. Most members of this group grow to 8-12 inches but can weigh up to 13 lbs. They are very rare as they live in extremely deep water, about 13,000 ft below the sea's surface. Dumbo Octopuses can withstand very cold temperatures and the total darkness that comes with life on the sea floor. Since there are very few predators that might eat them, this species does not have an ink sac.

The Dumbo is the deepest-dwelling species of octopus that we have ever discovered.

MIMIC OCTOPUS

The Mimic Octopus is a great example of how the science of studying octopuses is always changing and evolving. As the oceans are large and vast, this species was only just discovered in

1998, just off the coast of Indonesia. They are mid-sized octopuses, around 2 feet long.

The Mimic Octopus is a genius example of one of the octopus' best weapons of defense —*disguise!*

This octopus can transform itself to look and act like other animals or "*mimic*" them. The octopus does this to hide and blend into its surroundings and escape predators who might like a tasty octopus lunch. The Mimic Octopus has been known to pretend to be shrimp, sea snakes, and flatfish.

Can you imagine if you were able to change not only the color but the shape of your body as well? *It's pretty incredible!*

BLANKET OCTOPUS

By this point, you surely understand that some octopuses can be huge and some tiny. *But did you know that size difference doesn't just occur among different species?* Some, like the Blanket Octopus, have immense size diversity among males and females. Male blankets are pretty tiny, whereas the females can be ginormous!

Male Blanket Octopuses are only 1 inch in size. This is about as tiny as an octopus can get. *But the females?* **They can grow up to a whopping 6**

feet! A male Blanket Octopus weighs 40,000 times less than a female. This is the greatest size difference between genders in one species in the whole animal world.

But if we set the crazy size difference aside, there is another reason this species is also pretty cool. Female Blanket Octopuses have fleshy tissue that connects their legs. When they are swimming in the water, this looks almost like see-through pink fabric which blankets their limbs as they move. This helps disguise the actual size of these octopuses and makes them look even larger and scarier than they are to any predators lurking around.

Just one other reason this species deserves to be on this list!

COCONUT OCTOPUS

This species of octopus is a favorite for its beautiful dark color and long black arms lined with pearly white suckers. The Coconut Octopus, like the fruit in their name, can be found hiding in coconut shells that fall into the tropical pacific waters it calls home. They tend to live in deep waters and love to make their dens out of the old shells, even trying out different shells or moving them until they find the right fit and location.

As you might have guessed, the Coconut Octopus is one of the smaller species of octopus, only growing to 3 inches long with an arm span of 6 inches. However, don't let their small size fool you. These little guys are full of cool tricks, such as burying themselves entirely in the mud or sand if they need to hide and leaving only their eyes uncovered. But that isn't the coolest trick they can do.

The Coconut Octopus can actually walk on two legs, just like we do, although underwater, of course. *That's right!* Coconut Octopuses are able to walk with 2 of their arms, an ability they seem to share with only 1 other octopus species. *Pretty amazing!*

OCTOPUS WOLFI

This tiny octopus species is the smallest of all the known octopuses in the world. Measuring in at only 1 inch long, smaller than a walnut, and weighing just one gram, the Octopus Wolfi is a miniature mollusk about as heavy as just a single raisin. *This tiny species has big fan appeal.* Who wouldn't want to see a tiny octopus that could fit in a doll-sized aquarium or perch on the end of your finger?

Living in the Western Pacific waters, the Octopus Wolfi, also called the Star-Sucker Pygmy Octopus, lives in shallow water, merely 10 to 100 feet under the surface. They feed on small crustaceans and shellfish.

Sadly, these small octopuses also have a small life span of only 6 months.

CARIBBEAN REEF OCTOPUS

We're not saying we've left the best until last, but perhaps, we have left the most beautiful, intelligent, and amazing octopus until last.

The Caribbean Reef Octopus is the true ninja master when it comes to hiding in plain sight. This species can not only change color, but they can do it in an instant and seemingly disappear right before your eyes!

But that isn't all that makes these octopuses amazing.

The Caribbean Reef Octopus can control their skin and muscles to match the texture and feel of the coral or whatever else they are hiding against. With the help of their special color-changing cells called chromatophores, this species is almost impossible to find when blending into its background. This is a good thing because they are hunted by sharks who are only too happy to find a chewy octopus snack.

This astonishing creature lives in the balmy waters off the coast of South Florida, the Caribbean Islands, and the northern coast of South America. They are nocturnal, which means they sleep during the day and go out to hunt at night. They like to feast on crabs, clams, snails, and lobsters.

Now you are familiar with eight of the most fascinating octopus species in the world. *Which one is your favorite?* **It's hard to pick just one!**

FLOPPY SEA SPIDER!

HISTORY OF THE OCTOPUS

Modern-day octopuses evolved from a larger group of prehistoric cephalopods called **Muensterelloidea**. Whew... *that's a long name!* This group lived in the Jurassic and Cambrian periods and also included prehistoric squids. Like some species today, these prehistoric octopuses made their home in coastal waters and lived on the ocean floor.

Historical evidence of these early octopuses is rare because there are hardly any **fossils** to be found. *Without a shell or bone structure, there is not much to create a fossil.*

FUN FACT: Fossils are remains of skeletons, and even molds of skeletons, imprinted on the earth. After millions of years, these remains are *petrified* – essentially, turned into hardened rock. Given the octopus has no skeleton, most come and go, and we may never have known they even existed.

However, a few bits and bobs of octopus fossils have been found over the years. *What they revealed has been mind-boggling!*

Compared to other groups, octopuses seem to evolve super slowly. In the 300 to 500 million years they have been around, they don't seem to have changed much at all. Current thinking is that octopuses *(and squid and other cephalopods)* may evolve differently than most other species.

WHY DID THE OCTOPUS CROSS THE REEF?

To get to the other tide!

CHARACTERISTICS AND APPEARANCE

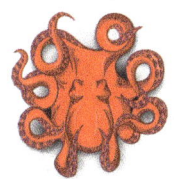

Can you imagine a cow suddenly turning green to blend in with the grass or changing its body shape to look like a goat? What about fitting itself through a hole the size of a mailbox? Or spraying out a cloud of milk to use as a decoy as it ran away? **That would be pretty crazy, right?!**

It's hard to imagine any other animal doing everything an octopus can do.

Because an octopus's body is made up of soft tissue and no bones, it can contort, stretch, and change its shape. Even a large species of octopus can fit its entire body through a hole the size of a quarter!

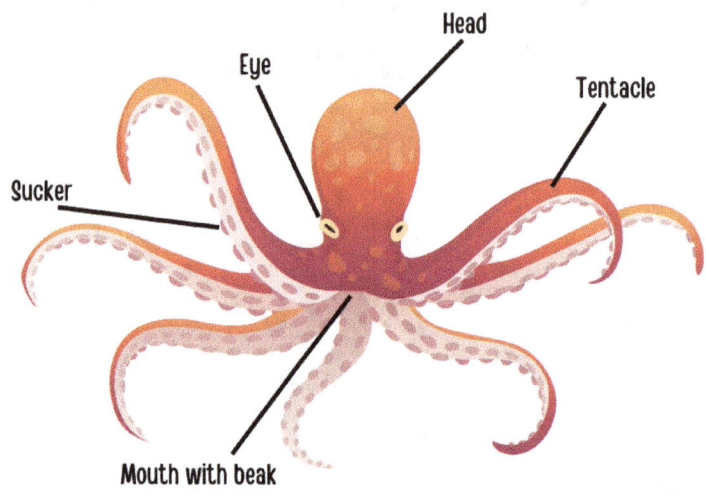

An octopus has two large eyes and a mouth with a hard beak. The mouth is not found on the "*face*" of the octopus but actually underneath the main body section at the center of the arms.

While you have red blood that is iron-based, an octopus has blue blood. This is because their blood is based on copper, which makes it a different color. Octopuses evolved to copper-based blood because it's better at circulating the oxygen around in their body at low temperatures, such as in the cold water of the ocean.

As you probably know, octopuses have eight arms with rows of suckers on the underside of each arm. These suckers not only grab things and anchor the octopus to surfaces, but they are also used to taste and smell. The suckers are very sophisticated and will not suction to their own skin, which is probably a good thing. Otherwise, an octopus might get all tangled up!

Their arms are quite amazing too. They can move in any direction, bend at any part, or even become stiff if needed. A few species of octopus can even "*walk*" with two of their arms along rocks and the sea floor.

ESCAPING PREDATORS

To a predator like a shark or a seal, an octopus is basically a tasty treat wrapped in a squishy body. Hiding and escape are the only defenses an octopus has.

Think about it! Octopuses don't have a hard shell like a clam or an armadillo. They don't have claws or sharp teeth to fight like a cat.

Octopuses must rely on their ability to outsmart their enemies through camouflage and other means of escape.

One way octopuses fool predators is by blending into their surroundings and hiding in plain sight. No other animal has the same ability to blend in and mimic its surroundings so quickly and accurately. Researchers are still learning how these animals do this since some species seem to be color-blind.

One theory is that octopuses use proteins called opsins in the skin, which react to wavelengths of light and use this information to decide what color to change into. It is probable that the skin responds on its own, automatically, and does not rely on the eyes at all.

Another way octopuses escape predators is by using their ink sacs. Most species of octopus squirt dark ink that clouds up the water and allows them to escape. The ink also has a bad taste which further discourages predators from following them. It can also impair sight, taste, and smell, which allows the octopus to get away undetected.

Octopuses also use colorful changes to warn predators and confuse them. This is called **deimatic behavior**, *doing something to startle a predator*. Octopuses may flash bright colors to alert the predator they are poisonous, or they might mimic the look of another dangerous and venomous animal, like a sea snake. It's not hard to see why this defense mechanism works so well. Imagine if a banana you were about to pick up suddenly flashed bright colors and turned into a snake. **You'd run a million miles!**

By surprising and confusing their predators with dazzling displays, octopuses can throw off their enemies and escape close encounters. Thankfully, octopuses can also swim very fast, propelling themselves with their arms to safety. This combination of confusion and speedy getaway helps octopuses escape from smart and swift predators like sharks.

THERE'S A GENIUS IN TOWN

Octopuses are very smart animals. Their large brains and complex nervous system make them superbly intelligent. But they aren't just *"brainy,"* as in not all their decision-making happens in their brains. Some of their brain power is spread out into their arms as well.

This is why octopuses are considered to have nine brains. Not only do they have a powerful brain in their heads, but each tentacle has its own brain-like receptors and can act independently from its head brain.

Octopuses are *so* intelligent they can navigate mazes, play games, use tools, and remember things quite well. Individual octopuses even seem to have their own personalities, habits, and quirks.

Some species have adapted to using the trash in the oceans to their advantage. They have created dens out of barrels, glass jars, and other debris. At least they are taking the *"reuse and recycle"* message to heart and turning something negative, like ocean trash, into something useful. Still, there is a danger to octopuses using human trash, such as cuts from broken glass or chemicals from old car batteries.

One study highlighted just how smart these animals are. It was performed on an octopus in captivity. The researchers wanted to know if an octopus could remember people's faces and recognize differences between individuals even through aquarium glass. For a set period of time, two different researchers came and saw the octopus every day. They dressed the same, were both men, and had similar hair color and style, etc. One man came to the octopus every day and gave it a treat. The other man came to the octopus and bothered it with a stick. He didn't hurt the octopus, but he did annoy it!

After just a week, the octopus would come to the man with the treats as soon as he showed up but would hide when he saw the man who annoyed him. This seemed to suggest octopuses can tell the difference between different people and remember their faces.

WHAT DO OCTOPUSES EAT?

If you were to walk into an octopus restaurant *or maybe swim in*, what kinds of foods might you find?

As there are over 300 species of octopuses, the menu is fairly wide. Octopuses spend a lot of time hiding from predators who want to eat them, but they are also predators of other animals. Octopuses enjoy all kinds of smaller animals, including sea stars, larval crabs, lobsters, sea snails, shrimp, fish, crabs, mollusks, clams, and sometimes other octopuses too. Some species also eat plants like kelp that grow in the ocean.

You may be wondering how a squishy and soft animal like an octopus eats such hard animals like clams and crabs. *Don't they have tough shells to get into?* This is a great question.

Octopuses may not have utensils as we do, but they do have some "*tools*" to use when getting into tougher prey. One trick they use is injecting paralyzing saliva into crabs before taking them apart with their hard, bird-like beaks to eat them. Octopuses have toxic venom they can use for this kind of occasion. For mollusks like clams, a nerve toxin is injected into the clam, and then the octopus's saliva slowly dissolves the shell. This may take a few hours. The clam then dies, and the octopus eats it.

A few species of octopus swallow their prey whole, but most eat with their **radula**, which is kind of like a small tongue covered in little teeth that can be used for scraping.

WHERE DO OCTOPUSES LIVE?

As you probably already know, you aren't likely to stumble across an octopus on your way to school or the grocery store. *But where **can** you find these fascinating marine animals?*

Octopuses can be found in every ocean of the world. Some octopuses live in shallow, coastal waters, while others live deep, deep down at the very bottom of the ocean. Some species prefer the warm waters of the Caribbean, and others the chilly waters of the Pacific Northwest United States.

Even octopuses that live in coastal areas are difficult to spot. While you might have seen a seal or even a whale or a shark, octopuses are rarely seen by people. One reason is that octopuses don't need to come to the surface of the water the way some other species do. Another reason is octopuses spend much of their time hanging out or hiding in their dens or houses.

Octopuses make their dens in coral reefs and rocky areas, finding small holes and crevices to live in. Sometimes octopuses even move rocks to build their den just how they want it. A few smaller species use shells as a den. Octopuses are very resourceful and live under and around the base of water bridges, in old discarded barrels, and in other trash thrown into the water by humans. Young octopuses can sometimes be found living in tide pools.

Most octopuses prefer to live alone and have their own territories they stay in. However, scientists are now discovering some species may be pretty social. There have been discoveries of larger groups of octopuses living together, which is surprising.

There is still much to learn about these amazing animals!

WHAT SEA CREATURES SAY HELLO 16 TIMES?

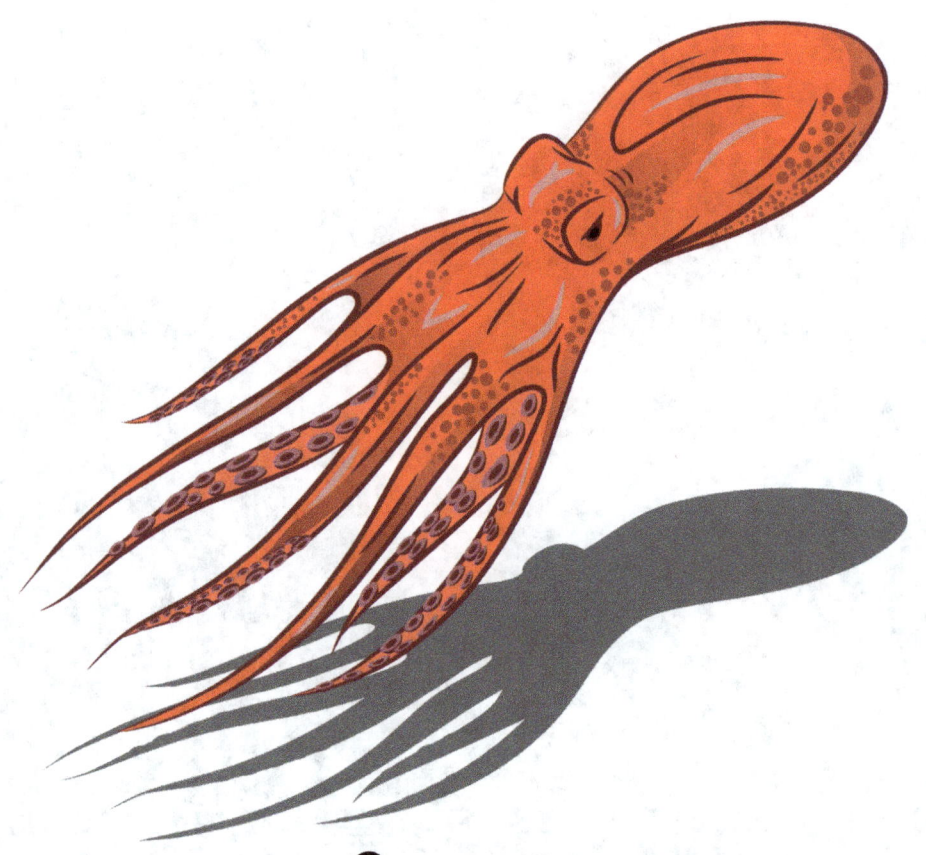

2 octopuses shaking hands!

THE LIFE CYCLE OF AN OCTOPUS

Did you know a hamster probably lives longer than the average octopus? It's true! While most hamsters live 2-3 years, the average octopus will go through its whole life in just 1-2 years.

Thankfully, much of an octopus' life is devoted to protecting and conserving its species. Although almost all the octopus species mate just once, a female octopus can lay anywhere from 10,000 to 200,000 eggs in that one mating. The average amount depends on the species.

But laying lots of eggs isn't the end of it, at least not for the female. Male octopuses die soon after mating, yet females live long enough to see the babies thrive.

The ocean is a tough place to be an egg, and the octopus mother knows this all too well. After mating with a male, the mother octopus carries the fertilized eggs until it is time to lay them. When she lays the eggs, she painstakingly cares for them by protecting them from predators, cleaning algae off the eggs, and never leaving their side.

Mother octopuses do not eat for the 2 to 10 months it takes for the eggs to hatch, which is something that depends on the species. After the eggs finally hatch, the mother uses her last energy to blow the hatchlings out of the den and on their way. When the tiny octopuses hatch, they can already swim, eat, and release their ink. The mother will then die soon after sending her young out into the world. She usually dies close to her den.

Why do octopuses die so young? Some scientists believe the short life span of octopuses may exist to ensure the seas do not become overpopulated.

Most octopus species hatch out as paralarvae, a kind of immature version of adult octopuses. They float along the surface with the plankton and eat things like zooplankton. These tiny octopuses may stay in this stage for a few weeks to a few months.

If they survive this stage, the young octopuses fall down to the ocean floor, where they live as they grow into adult octopuses. There are a few species that hatch out babies that are already fully-formed octopuses, only smaller, but most start life this way.

The odds of a newly-hatched octopus making it to adulthood aren't great. With so many predators eager for a mini-octopus meal, not many of the hatchlings will survive. In fact, probably only 1% of hatchlings will make it to full adulthood! This means that out of 10,000, only 100 survive.

Thankfully, only two octopuses are needed to replace the lost parents, so the species can still thrive.

Unlike many other animals, octopuses are not currently endangered or at risk of extinction. However, rising temperatures and levels of the ocean, trash, and other environmental problems do affect many species.

It is important for all of us to care for our oceans and the amazing animals that live hidden from our sight.

BEFRIEND OCTOPUSES!

We hope you have loved diving into the colorful and ever-changing world of octopuses with us. These fascinating creatures are one of the ocean's continually unfolding mysteries, and we're so glad you came along on this adventure!

If you would like to be a friend to octopuses, visit and support your local aquarium and marine societies, which are wonderful resources for learning more about these amazing creatures and ocean life.

And remember: recycling, buying only what you need, and reusing what you can all help to keep trash out of the oceans and create a world that cares for all life, including octopuses.

THANK YOU!

Thank you for reading this book and for allowing us to share our love of octopuses with you!

If you've enjoyed this book, please let us know by leaving a rating and a brief review wherever you made your purchase! This helps us spread the word to other readers!

Thank you for your time, and have an awesome day!

For more information, please visit:

www.animalreads.com

© Copyright 2023 - All rights reserved Admore Publishing

ISBN: 978-3-96772-137-9

ISBN: 978-3-96772-138-6

ISBN: 978-3-96772-139-3 (*Ebook*)

Animal Reads at www.animalreads.com

The content contained within this book may not be reproduced, duplicated or transmitted without direct written permission from the author or the publisher.

Under no circumstances will any blame or legal responsibility be held against the publisher, or author, for any damages, reparation, or monetary loss due to the information contained within this book. Either directly or indirectly.

Published by Admore Publishing: Gotenstraße, Berlin, Germany

www.admorepublishing.com

www.ingramcontent.com/pod-product-compliance
Lightning Source LLC
LaVergne TN
LVHW020142080526
838202LV00048B/3992